CW00434211

ICE

ICE

❧

PHOTOGRAPHS BY MARZENA POGORZAŁY

WITH REFLECTIONS BY ANNE MICHAELS

For Gordon, with best wishes –

Marzena

April 2015

Published by The Cuckoo Press for John Sandoe (Books) Ltd
10 Blacklands Terrace, London SW3 2SR

Photographs © Marzena Pogorzały

A CIP catalogue reference for this book is available from the British Library

ISBN: 978 0 9566444 6 6

Design and cover illustration by Fenella Willis

Printed and bound in the UK by CPI Group (UK) Ltd, Croydon CR0 4YY

There was something about them so slumberous and so pure, so massive and yet so evanescent, so majestic in their cheerless beauty, without, after all, any of the salient points which give character to description, that they seemed to me material for a dream, rather than things to be definitely painted in words...

DR ELISHA KENT KANE on icebergs, 1853

Marzena Pogorzały has been photographing polar ice for over twenty years. Trained as a marine biologist and oceanographer, she first went to Svalbard archipelago in the Arctic Circle on the invitation of the Polish Academy of Sciences in 1992. The elemental, almost abstract landscape made such a deep impression on her that planning subsequent visits became something of an obsession. Five more expeditions to North and South polar regions followed, and icebergs have remained the object of her visual and intellectual fascination. Her finest images were produced on board ice patrol ship HMS Endurance and from the vantage point of its Lynx helicopters in 1999 and 2007.

Marzena's work has drawn widespread praise. Al Alvarez has written of 'her steady, loving eye' and 'faultless sense of composition'. Neal Ascherson considers her 'one of the most distinguished and original polar photographers of her generation', with a 'vigilant instinct for the numinous'. Simon Schama has described her subject matter as 'sculpture that isn't sculpture – liquid, solid, monumental' and her images as 'startling works of art – haunting, powerful, mesmerising'.

Her work has featured in many publications including *Geographical*, *The New York Review of Books*, *British Journal of Photography*, *The Independent Magazine* and

Portfolio magazine. Her ice photographs have been exhibited by the Royal Geographical Society, London (1998), Ffotogallery, Cardiff (2000), and Ice House Gallery, London (2005), as well as during the 2006 Antarctic Treaty Consultative Meeting in Edinburgh.

She has been assisted in her project by the Polar Regions Section of the Foreign and Commonwealth Office, the Royal Navy, the UK Antarctic Heritage Trust, the Polish Cultural Institute in London, Kodak and the Argentine Navy.

Marzena works at John Sandoe (Books) Ltd in London.

REFLECTIONS

The lines of a drawing both separate and bind. Every line is a horizon between one object and another, or one state of matter and another: between flesh and air, land and sea, smoke and sky. So the polar light and its lines of shadow give form to the ice. The ice is frozen change, passive and animate, sculpted by light. Hard as stone, mutable as flesh.

The ice is antipodal; each edge of brilliance or blackness defines a landscape of opposing forces, symbiotic in their opposition. The lines that separate and bind: light and dark, endeavour and futility, will and fate, ambition and surrender, communion and terror, dream and nightmare, desire and regret, epiphanies of loneliness and the deepest human bonds of loyalty and ideals. The sharpness of ice, the softness of snow. The ghostly effects of light without heat.

And in these extremes, the polar light sculpts time as well as space. Ice, sky, and sea merge, separate, solidify. Brilliant or blackened, a shifting palette, the polar landscape forms and re-forms; impermanent and vulnerable, yet seemingly immortal and immutable. To this landscape of desolate, gargantuan proportion we bring our human sense of time and scale. Headlong, at high speed, our mortality confronts geologic slowness; the reckoning of a single perishable life in relation to eternity. A photograph can witness this confrontation, this reckoning. A photograph can record this moment of impossible, ecstatic balance: between an intensity of vision and the immensity of time.

And the photographer herself, invisible, is the human presence in the uninhabited landscape.

★

The ice is frozen moonlight, frozen starlight. It floats between the black sea and the black sky. A grandeur, one immensity calved from another, and yet, monumentally susceptible; the fate of ice is water. The great age of the ice is slowly being eaten by salinity, warmer waters, the albedo. When the ice is gone, it will be remembered by the massive ecological consequences that follow.

Within the ice are pockets of ancient air by which we can measure, with radio-metric dating, the slow breath of the noble gas krypton and its half-life of 230,000 years. As the ice recedes, frozen life will be revealed and revived: moss, inert for thousands of years, regrown in a lab.

The ice may come to represent all that is best and worst of human striving: staggering moments of endurance and awe; and the irrevocable consequences of human ambition. Remnants of immensity.

★

In dispossession, in bitter and bitten shadows and compacted light, in bone-freezing cold, there is the last expansive evening in the summer garden, the last July afternoon drive, a moment across a table set with lanterns, on the lawn.

Moments when a single word was rescue; and moments of regret, error, indecision, mistrust, the half-life of love.

Perhaps there is nothing hungrier than memory.

The polar explorers, starving, dreamed of roast beef and chocolate; the feel of an apple in the hand. In their howling tent, rigid with cold, they dreamed of heaped plates, and of the green of an English lane, hot baths and the sight and song of birds. They dreamed the way a sailor dreams of land.

But there are also those who – in the rainy morning, in the endless heat of a congested city, in the soft summer dusk – dream of ice.

ANNE MICHAELS, 2014

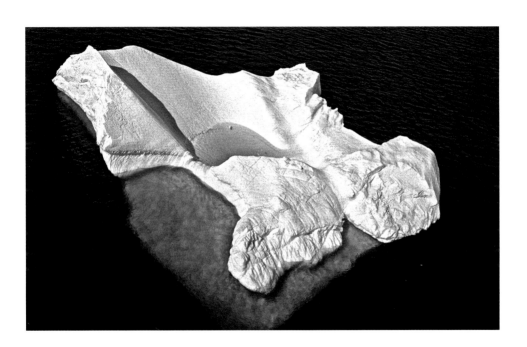

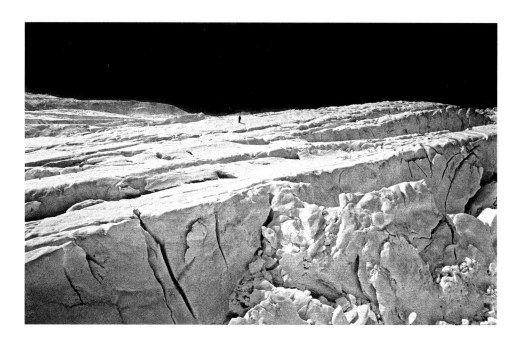